I0428191

The Gift Of Confidence

Crack The Code Of Self Confidence And Achieve Success In Your Workplace And Your Personal Life

Table of Contents

Introduction

This book contains proven steps and strategies on how to be more confident. This book will help you improve your belief in yourself and eventually achieve great success in life.

If you are one of those people who are insecure, unmotivated, socially inept, underachieving, and negative, you may be suffering from low self-confidence and self-esteem. Low self-confidence can be dangerous. It can destroy your relationships, keep you from accepting great career opportunities, and prevent you from experiencing true love and intimacy. If you have low self-confidence, you will constantly feel frustrated. You regularly belittle yourself and your abilities. You do not strive for a better life because you think you do not deserve it.

This book will help you improve your personal life and achieve success in your chosen career by building your self-confidence. This book will help you recognize your worth and build confidence in yourself and your abilities. Your life will change for the better.

Chapter 1 - Understanding Confidence

What is Confidence?

Self-confidence enables you to have a positive but realistic perception about yourself, your abilities and your circumstances. When you are confident with yourself, you are not afraid to take challenges and face your problems. When you are confident, you stand up for what you believe in.

Self-confidence is just a perception, but it can be a self-fulfilling prophecy. When you are confident with yourself, you believe in your ability to succeed in your chosen field.

Development of Self-confidence

There are several factors that affect the development of self-confidence. How children feel about themselves is heavily dependent on how their parents treat them. When parents provide unconditional love and acceptance, their children generally feel good about themselves. If you had parents who were extremely demanding or critical, then you may believe you are incapable of success. If your parents constantly invalidated you, then it will be harder for you to like yourself.

Self-confidence or lack of it usually starts in childhood. When parents discourage independence and self-reliance, their children will doubt their abilities and capability. Lack of self-confidence does not necessarily mean you lack the ability. Confidence is just a perception that is influenced by the people around you during your development years.

There are other factors that impact confidence. Some of these factors are social standing, level of education, job security, health, and actual intelligence.

Signs of Low Self-confidence

Many people suffer from low self-confidence. People with low self-confidence often go through their lives constantly intimidated and feeling insecure. They think they are not good enough. They think they do not deserve success. If you think you are one of these people, then read on for the other signs and symptoms of low confidence.

1. People Pleasing Habit

Individuals who have low self-esteem often seek approval from others. They sacrifice too much, even their own needs, to make other people happy. They take good care of other people while neglecting their own needs. People with poor self-confidence believe other people's approval is the main source of happiness.

2. Unable to Accept Compliments Graciously

People without self-confidence cannot accept compliments graciously. They feel uncomfortable when receiving kind words and compliments from other people. They respond to compliments using self-deprecating statements like "it was easy," "it's nothing," or "I just got lucky."

3. Poor Personal Boundaries

Timid people often feel guilty when they say "no." They feel obligated to give in to requests, even if they are not comfortable with them. They often put other people's needs ahead of their own.

4. Feeling Guilty When Good Things Happen

People who are unsure of themselves often expect bad things to happen, so they feel uncomfortable when good things happen.

4. Reactive

People who have extreme self-doubt do not feel like they control any situations. They think other people are always the source of authority, power and judgment. People with low self-confidence are also quick to react to criticism. What other people say or do affects them heavily.

5. Unable to Handle Criticism and Rejection

People with poor self-confidence take rejection and criticism personally. They find rejection and criticism hurtful. Because they fear criticism and rejection, individuals with low self-confidence avoid challenging tasks and delay tasks they think they cannot do.

6. Afraid to Ask Questions

Shy and timid people accept everything at face value. Because of this, they are open to manipulation and deceit. They participate in an activity or a cause without having sufficient information.

Importance of Confidence

1. Confidence is important in relationships.

Confidence is more important in relationships than physical beauty or attractiveness. In a recent research, both men and women said they prefer confidence over physical beauty. People who confidently smile at them often catch their attention. Confident people have better relationships because they have less insecurity about themselves. They are also more loving, honest and open.

2. Confidence is essential in career mobility.

Self-confident people get promoted more often than people with low self-esteem. They are not afraid to take risks, and they believe in themselves and their abilities. They often have better job performance, higher standards, and greater career ambitions.

3. Confidence generates trust.

Most people tend to trust confident people right away. In your subconscious mind, confidence is equal to competence. The subconscious mind does not distinguish perceptions and reality. Self-confidence generates trust. You have to project trustworthiness. To do this, you have to project confidence.

4. Confidence builds resilience.

When you are confident, you will be less disappointed when someone rejects you. Your confidence prevents you from losing hope when things do not go as planned.

5. Confidence influences happiness.

Lack of self-confidence can cause many problems such as eating disorders, poor body image, alcohol abuse, drug abuse, depression and anxiety. Low self-confidence also causes people to isolate themselves or even bully others. Confidence and happiness are closely correlated.

6. Confidence enables you to be comfortable in your own skin.

People who have self-confidence are attractive. They light up the room. Confident people are proud of who they are. They are comfortable in their own skin and feel good enough.

6. Confidence cultivates leadership skills.

Self-confident employees usually hold leadership roles. Confidence allows you to influence others and make a difference in other people's lives.

Confidence is an important trait. It is an essential ingredient for success, happiness, and a life well lived.

Chapter 2 - Characteristics Of A Confident Person

Many psychologists say that confidence is more important than competence. Self-confidence has the power to bring you unlimited success. It serves as a fuel you can use to live your dreams.

1. Ambitious

People who have confidence in themselves and in their abilities have big dreams. They are ambitious. They are sure of what they want and work hard to get it.

2. Sociable

People with high self-confidence are sociable. They are at ease in different social situations. They can deal with people from all walks of life.

3. Self- Assured

Self-confident people are sure of themselves. They believe they are valuable and worthy. They have accepted who they are and do not have insecurities.

4. Risk Taking

People with high confidence are not afraid to take risks and face challenges. They are not afraid of rejection and the possibility of losing.

5. Competitive

People who are self-confident know their potential. This is the reason they love competition.

6. Self-love

Self-confident individuals love and accept themselves. They are satisfied with themselves, prioritize themselves, and practice healthy self-care.

4. Self-awareness

People with high self-confidence know they have weaknesses but are at peace with that fact. While acknowledging their limitations, they also recognize their potential. They are aware of their strengths and use their weaknesses as an advantage.

5. Persistent

Confident people are determined. They do not give up on their goals even when things get tough. Despite failure, they embrace the act of having tried in the first place.

6. Hardworking

People who are confident know hard work is necessary in achieving success in life. This is the reason they work hard. No matter how difficult or challenging the work is, they do their best in accomplishing each task assigned to them.

7. Tolerant

Confident individuals are the most tolerant and accepting people. They do not take other people's mistakes, shortcomings and behavior personally, and they are forgiving.

Confidence is usually built during the early years of a person's life, but it is not too late. You can still cultivate your own self-confidence, even in your adult years. In the next chapters, you learn how to develop confidence in yourself and reap its benefits.

Chapter 3 - Pay Attention To Internal Conversations

We talk to ourselves all the time – when we are eating, taking a bath, or even caught up in morning traffic. What do you constantly tell yourself? Does your internal conversation lift your spirit or does it bring you down? Does it make you feel good about yourself or does it increase self-doubt?

People with low self-confidence talk to themselves negatively all the time. They often say something like:

"I am not good enough."

"I am not attractive enough."

"My sister is better."

"I will not achieve great success."

"I will never get promoted."

"I cannot do that."

People with low self-esteem berate and insult themselves constantly. Internal conversation is very powerful, creating a vicious cycle if used in a negative way. An internal conversation has the power to influence your relationships, and it affects how you treat and perceive other people. It influences your grooming habits, your style of speech and the level of effort you put into every task.

To achieve great success at work and in life, you have to recognize that you are good enough. You must speak positively to yourself.

The first step to transforming yourself into a powerful, self-confident individual is to pay attention to how you talk to yourself. Take time to listen to what you say. Are you saying kind words or insulting and belittling words?

If you have low self-confidence, you probably say bad things to yourself. Once you realize you are having self-defeating conversations with yourself, it is time to change.

Here is how you can replace negative self-talk with more positive words:

1. Silence your inner critic and eliminate negative chatter.

   As mentioned earlier, the first step in developing positive self-talk is awareness. You have to be aware of your thoughts and buried emotions. Anger, guilt, resentment and bitterness fuel negative self-talk. Once you become aware of the negative emotions you have carried all these years, you can more easily silence your inner critic and eliminate negative self-talk.

   Visualize a small box in your mind, and put all your negative thoughts about yourself into the box. The next time you have a negative thought about yourself, take a deep breath and quickly eliminate it by placing it in the imaginary box.

   Another way to silence your inner critic is to give it a name. This sounds silly, but it is an effective technique. You can call your inner critic "Nagger,"

"Perfectionist," or plain "Critic." Each time a negative thought enters your mind, you can just tell your inner "Critic" to be quiet.

2. Accept your imperfections.

Perfectionism is often a product of low self-confidence and low self-esteem, and people use it to overcompensate for the perceived inadequacy. You have to stop holding yourself to unrealistically high standards. Accept that you have limitations, and it is okay to make mistakes sometimes. No one is perfect, and your best is good enough.

3. Rephrase negative statements.

To effectively eliminate negative thoughts, you have to rephrase them. Instead of saying "I am fat," say something like "I have the willpower to exercise regularly." Instead of saying "I am a loser," say something like "I have the ability to change my situation and my destiny."

4. Stay away from social media.

Many studies show that social media and social networking sites increase the levels of self-criticism. Instead of appreciating other people's beautiful and fabulous lives, take time to appreciate your own beauty and your own life. Pay attention to your thoughts and feelings. Say kind words to yourself. When you stay away from social networking site, you stop comparing your life to other people's lives and start appreciating yourself more.

5. Treat yourself like your own best friend.

If you ever catch yourself in a self-deprecating tirade, ask yourself, "What would my best friend tell me in this situation?" Be your own best friend and your own cheerleader. Avoid saying bad things about yourself, and become your own friend.

6. Say positive affirmations.

Affirmations have the power to reprogram your subconscious mind and replace negative self-belief with positive self-belief. They empower you and allow you to open yourself to more opportunities. By repeating affirmations, you plant positive thoughts into your subconscious mind, which helps you elevate your life to the next level. Affirmations also make you feel good about yourself.

It is best to write down positive affirmations before you say them. Make sure your affirmations are in the present tense. Use affirmations you feel comfortable with.

Once your affirmations are ready, read each one out loud. Make sure you say them with conviction and strong faith. It also helps if you smile while saying your affirmations.

Remember to say your affirmations at least twice per day. Affirmations are not a quick fix. You have to say these affirmations consistently to reap the optimal results.

Here are some affirmations you can use to increase your self-confidence:

"I embrace confidence and let go of my shyness."

"I am self-reliant."

"I am enthusiastic and energetic."

"I am healthy, well-groomed, and confident."

"Nothing is impossible."

"I love change."

"I can adapt to any situation."

"I am unique."

"I accept myself completely."

"I love myself."

"I love challenges."

"I choose to be happy every day."

"Life is fun."

"I believe in myself."

"Life is rewarding."

"I am passionate, and I am inspired."

"I am flexible."

"I am successful."

"I trust myself."

"I have unlimited power."

"I have star quality, and I will shine."

"I feel great."

"Today will be a wonderful day."

"Everything will be fine."

"I will be successful".

"I treat everyone with respect."

"I am persistent."

Affirmations help to quiet your inner critic and improve your internal conversations. You talk to yourself all day long, and these conversations can make or break your day. In fact, these conversations can make or break your life.

Chapter 4 - Dress For Success

Confidence is a perception. If you want to succeed in life, you have to dress the part. If you want to project intelligence and confidence, then you have to dress sharply. If you look good, you will also feel good. Dressing well boosts your confidence, strength, and self-belief. It can also help improve other people's perceptions about you.

Here are some tips on projecting confidence by dressing for success:

1. Choose comfortable clothes.

Comfort is the primary consideration in choosing the right clothes for you. If you wear comfortable clothes, you feel more relaxed and more confident.

2. Buy basic clothing pieces needed for power dressing.

Power dressing is a style or type of clothing, make-up, and hairstyle intended to make people look competent and authoritative. Power dressing is usually required in the fields of government, law, and business. Here are some of the pieces that you will need if you want to power dress:

For men

Dark and conservative suits in charcoal, black, or navy blue – These suits make you look authoritative and smart.

A good pair of jeans – If you want to look smart and confident, even in casual clothes, then you have to invest in a few pairs of quality jeans. Go for classic cuts when choosing the right pair of jeans.

Black Leather Shoes- Black leather shoes are perfect for work, but be sure to keep your shoes polished and clean if you want to look smart.

Loafers – Loafers go with casual and semi-formal clothing. If you want to look smart and confident, then invest in a pair of loafers.

Quality Shirts – You must invest in high quality shirts. These shirts last for a long time. Choose classic shirts with neutral colors as they do not go out of style.

For Women

The LBD – The little black dress will never be outdated. The LBD is perfect for work, cocktail parties, and dates.

Pumps – If you want to look confident and smart, then you should invest in a good pair of pumps.

Suit – If you want to be respected at work, then you need to dress the part. Wearing a suit makes you look powerful and authoritative.

Pearl Earrings – Pearl earrings are classic. Wearing them instantly adds class to your outfit.

Leather bags – You do not have to own a Hermes bag, but you should have a decent leather bag. Leather bags are good investments because they are durable and never go out of style.

A classic pair of jeans – You have to get the perfect pair of jeans that fits well and compliments your body form. A good pair of jeans goes with any other type of clothing.

3. Your clothes must be well pressed.

Wearing crumpled clothes speak volumes about how you feel about yourself. When you wear well-pressed clothes, you show your boss and colleagues that you are confident and you mean business. It also means you are concerned about the way you look. If you do not take care of yourself and how you look, then you cannot expect to be trusted with bigger responsibilities.

4. Prepare in advance.

Whether you are going to a job interview, a client presentation, or town hall meeting, always dress to impress. When you look good, you will feel confident. In order to do this, you have to prepare in advance. Make sure to prepare what you are going to wear the night before. This ensures a polished and confident look.

5. Dress for the role that you want.

Do you want to be a CEO, a corporate attorney, or a successful entrepreneur? You have to dress like one! Your personal appearance has a big effect on your future income opportunities. You have to build your image if you want your confidence and your business to grow. Observe how CEOs, lawyers and other successful people dress, and follow their lead.

6. Get a makeover.

When you look great, you will feel great. Get a new hair color and use makeup that accentuates your features. Invest in good hair care and skin care products. When you look good, you will be more confident.

7. Do not wear flashy jewelry.

Flashy jewelry like a big diamond ring is tacky. You do not want to look like Snoop Dogg or Kanye West. A pair of small diamond stud earrings and a classic watch are enough. You can also wear a simple gold or silver necklace.

Remember that you are what you wear. To project confidence, you have to look your best. When you dress the part, you are almost half way to success at work and in life.

Chapter 5 - Be Resilient

To become more confident in your abilities, you have to be resilient. Everyone is going through a hard time in life. In fact, adversity and challenges are vital parts of human life. Many people doubt their abilities when faced with problems and adversities. For many people, it is hard to be confident after losing a job or a painful divorce.

Resiliency is simply the ability to bounce back after a misfortune. Confident people are known to be resilient. Resiliency is one of the core components of confidence.

Here are some tips and techniques to help you become more resilient:

1. Be flexible.

Confident and resilient people have accepted the fact that challenges and problems are part of life. They find ways to adapt to adversities. They are ready to adjust their goals and plans if needed. To develop resiliency, you have to be willing to change.

2. Keep your sense of humor.

There is always something funny in every situation, even in times of adversity. Playful humor improves your ability to survive and overcome an unfortunate event. When you laugh in spite of difficulty, you decrease the level of stress and anxiety. Many psychologists believe that humor is even more powerful than determination.

3. Be a survivor.

People who have great self-confidence do not consider themselves victims. They see themselves as survivors. They do not tell people victim stories, but instead, they tell success and survival stories.

4. Release your stress and tension.

When you are faced with adversity and other difficult situations, it is easy to give in to stress and tension. To develop resiliency, you have to learn how to release negative emotions. There are many ways you can do this. You can draw, paint, or write a journal. You can also talk to a friend, do yoga, or meditate.

5. Have a strong sense of purpose.

Confident individuals have a strong sense of purpose. They understand that everything happens for a reason. To develop resiliency, you have to find your purpose, even during difficult times. To illustrate this point, let's talk about the story of Erin. Her brother committed suicide for unknown reasons. Erin was devastated. She lost her optimism and confidence in herself, but she realized that life has to go on. She searched for meaning and found her new purpose.

She finally went out of the house again after locking herself up for two months. She started helping people who suffered from depression and suicidal tendencies. Erin might not have saved the life of her brother, but she saved many other lives. Because of this, she was able to live with the pain of losing her brother. She was able to move on and build a better, brighter life.

6. Learn the lessons of adversity.

To be resilient and confident, you have to look at difficult situations as opportunities to learn something new. Look at adversity as an opportunity to build a better life for yourself and for your loved ones. Adversity is a great teacher, so learn your lessons well.

7. Develop a strong support group.

To build up your resilience and self-confidence, you have to surround yourself with people who love and support you. Surround yourself with people who believe in you.

8. Develop your problem solving and critical thinking skills.

When you enhance your critical thinking skills, it is easier to rise above difficult situations. This also improves confidence.

9. Take action.

Take deliberate steps to improve your situation in your life. Action builds resiliency and confidence. When you face adversity head on, your confidence in yourself and your abilities will improve. It is also easier for you to move on if you take action.

When you successfully conquer adversity, you instantly feel better about yourself. When you conquer a difficult situation, it will be easier to believe in your abilities.

Chapter 6 - Be Optimistic

Optimism builds your self-confidence. It is a strong foundation of self-confidence. When you are an optimist, you feel good. When you feel good, you feel secure and confident in yourself.

Optimism ultimately makes you feel better about yourself. Not all of us are born optimists. In fact, if you suffer from low self-confidence and low self-esteem, you are most likely a pessimist. The good news is it is not too late to change. Optimism can be learned.

To help you cultivate optimism, promise yourself:

1. To be so strong that nobody can destroy your peace of mind.

2. To make all your friends feel special.

3. To talk positively about happiness, health, and abundance to every person you meet.

4. To be too big for petty worries and anxieties.

5. To look at the brighter side of things.

6. To forgive yourself for the mistakes you have made in the past.

7. To be happy for the success of other people.

8. To stay cheerful even in the most difficult situations.

9. To dedicate time for self-improvement.

10. To think only of the best outcome.

11.   To do my best at work.

12.   To be too noble for anger.

13.   To be ready for success.

When repeating this creed to yourself, you will eventually become an optimist and your self-confidence will drastically improve. These beliefs are powerful and can alter your subconscious mind for the better.

Aside from the "positivity creed," here are some additional tips to use for improving your optimism:

1. Cultivate thankfulness.

When you are grateful, you are more positive and confident. Remember, there is always something to be thankful for. You are more blessed than you think.

If you find it hard to be grateful, then keep a gratitude journal. Every morning right after you wake up, write down the things you are grateful for. Be grateful for your parents, your spouse, your children, your friends, your job, your car, and your home. Take time to appreciate your abilities and your talents. Appreciate all your blessings. When you take time to appreciate everything you have, you realize you are luckier than you think.

2. Control your responses.

It is not what happens to you but how you respond to it. You have very little control over what happens to you, but you can fully control how you react to it. Always choose to look at the bright side of every situation because every situation is an opportunity to succeed and grow.

3. Find the good in every situation.

Be a glass half-full kind of person. You have to find something positive even in difficult situations.

4. Think happy thoughts.

When you think happy thoughts, you instantly become happier no matter what your current circumstance is. When you have a habit of thinking happy thoughts, you create a sunny disposition and your relationships will improve.

Do not think too much about poverty and problems. Think about the possible solutions. No matter what your situation is right now, remember that there is always a rainbow after the storm.

5. Spend time with the people you like.

Spending a lot of time with people you really like can help you develop optimism even during tough times. It is easier to stay positive if you surround yourself with positive people.

6. Be generous.

Giving makes us happy. It even makes us happier than being on the receiving end. Generosity improves your self-confidence and self-esteem, and it helps you cultivate optimism.

7. Focus on the things you want.

Optimism is the core of the law of attraction. Many manifestation experts and spiritual mystics believe that whatever we focus on expands. This means that if we do positive deeds and focus on positive thoughts, we can attract great things in life. If you want to attract more money, then focus on abundance and not on the lack of it. If you want more happiness and self-confidence, then think thoughts that cultivate happiness, success, and self-confidence.

8. Create a positive and happy "movie" of your life.

As mentioned earlier, it is easy to play the victim. However, if you want to improve your self-confidence, then you have to highlight the positive things that happened in your life. Think of the time when you bought a car, got promoted, or traveled abroad. Remember that you are not a victim. You are more blessed than you think.

9. Identify any improvement in your current situation.

If your situation is improving, then you need to celebrate it. Remember that to achieve success, you have to take one step at a time. Any improvement, no matter how small, is worth celebrating.

Confidence and optimism are tightly linked. They go hand-in-hand. Without positivity and optimism, it is difficult to stay confident when faced with challenges and difficulty.

Chapter 7 - Love And Take Care Of Yourself

If you want to improve your self-confidence, then you have to first love and care for yourself. Self-love is another key part of confidence.

Most people find it hard to love themselves because they believe self-love is the same as selfishness. The truth is that self-love is not selfish. Loving yourself is not the same as being conceited, arrogant, or narcissistic. Loving yourself simply means that you care for yourself, respect yourself, and take time to get to know yourself intimately.

Self-love is an important ingredient for developing self-confidence and achieving success. Here are some ways to help you increase your self-love:

1. Acknowledge that you are a loving person who is worthy of love and success. Do not base your self-worth on other people's opinions. Accept yourself, and accept the fact that you are a valuable person.

2. Be compassionate with yourself. Take time to listen to your feelings and acknowledge them. Do not judge yourself for feeling the way you do. Gently acknowledge any negative feelings and release them.

3. Surround yourself with loving people. Choose to be around people who lift up your spirits. Stay away from people who constantly criticize you and put you down. If you want to develop confidence and increase your self-love, then be with positive people.

4. Be loving to the people around you. Everyone is fighting a hard battle, so it is crucial to be kind. When you treat others kindly, you like yourself more and your self-confidence improves.

5. Do something you are passionate about. It is not too late to find work that you truly love. You spend a lot of time at work, so make sure you enjoy it. If you are too stressed to eat or sleep, then it is a sign to find another job.

6. Create a work-life balance. You have to work hard to earn a living, but it is also important to play hard. Remember that your job is not everything. You can always find another job, but you cannot bring back the time spent overly focused on making money. Money makes your life comfortable, but it cannot make you happy. You have to engage in activities that make you happy.

7. Take care of yourself. If you want to increase your self-confidence and self-love, then you must take care of yourself. You can take great care of yourself in many ways, including:

    ⁉ Start your day with love – Most people check their phones or laptop first thing in the morning, and it is no wonder that they have already absorbed toxic thoughts and feelings so early in the morning. Start your day by affirming your value and your worth. Take a few deep breaths and drink a glass of lukewarm water. Take time to open your window and appreciate the sunrise. You can also start your day by listing all the things you are grateful for.

- Meditate – Take time to meditate. Meditation helps build self-confidence. It also helps ease stress and anxiety. You can even use it to control your mind and direct your thoughts.

- Try something new – When you expand your interests and try something new, you will feel more alive and confident in yourself.

- Eat healthy foods – Eliminate sugary drinks and desserts from your diet. Try to eat healthy foods such as oats, fruits, and vegetables. Make sure to consume vitamins, as well. When you nourish yourself, you are healthier. When you are healthy, you become more confident.

- Exercise – Any form of exercise instantly makes you feel good about yourself. Exercise helps control your weight, and when you look good, you feel good. Aside from its aesthetic purposes, exercise also helps combat many diseases. You can also boost your energy and improve your mood by exercising. Many studies show that regular exercise helps eliminate depression and anxiety.

- Do deeds that are aligned with your principles and values -When you maintain your integrity and stick with your principles, you feel better about yourself. Integrity is a very important component of self-confidence. It is difficult to like and be proud of yourself if you do things against your values.

⊹ Forgive yourself - If you have done something against your values, then you have to find the strength to forgive yourself. When you love and forgive yourself, you can move on more easily. Everybody makes mistakes, so do not be too hard on yourself.

⊹ Forgive other people – Once you have forgiven the people who have wronged you, you release yourself from all the anger and the bitterness. When you learn to forgive, you can live a more positive and happier life.

⊹ Have fun – Life is filled with challenges and difficulty. If you want to have a happier and more fulfilling life, then you have to incorporate fun and leisure into your daily schedule. Take time to crack jokes and play with your friends. Yes, adults need playtime, too. Sometimes, you just have to awaken your inner kid.

⊹ Read books that inspire you – Take time to read. When you read inspirational books or even blogs, it is easier to stay more positive, happy and confident.

⊹ Take care of your finances – If you want to take care of yourself, then you have to take care of your financial life. Remember to save – your future self will definitely thank you for it. Do not buy things you do not need just to enhance your self-image.

- Maintain a proper hygiene – To develop confidence and self-love, keep your body clean and presentable. Make it a habit to take a bath in the morning and at night before sleeping. Make it a habit to brush your teeth after eating. You also have to take care of your appearance. Moisturize your skin and exfoliate often.

- Get rest – To maintain great health, you have to rest when you are tired. You also have to get enough sleep every night. When you get enough sleep, you feel happier, healthier, and more energetic. You can also get a relaxing massage after a stressful day.

- Drink a lot of water – To increase your level of self-love, you need to drink a lot of water. When you keep yourself hydrated, your body will be healthier.

- Keep your home clean and tidy – Your home and personal space reflects and affects your mood and your disposition. Your home says a lot about you, so make sure it stays clean and well organized.

- Be in touch with the Divine – Even if you are not religious, take time to be spiritual. When you connect with the Divine, you feel more peaceful. As a result, you become more confident.

Self-love is essential for developing self-confidence. If you do not love and take care of yourself, feeling confident becomes very challenging. The love you give yourself is the most important kind of love you will ever receive.

Chapter 8 - Believe In Yourself

To develop self-confidence, you have to have a strong faith in yourself and your abilities. You must be your own biggest fan.

When you believe in yourself, you have better work performance and life satisfaction. Believing in yourself also boosts your determination and persistence. You will also feel more at ease in social situations, and you can cope with challenges more easily.

Here are some ways to strengthen your belief in yourself:

1. Identify your doubts and ease them.

To strengthen your faith in yourself, you have to identify your doubts and try hard to ease them. Put a red flag on the "I can't" and the "What ifs" and replace these with "I can" and "I will."

2. Do not listen to toxic people.

There are always going to be toxic people in your life – people who make you feel bad and put you down. Toxic people bring other people down to feel better about themselves, so it is important to avoid taking the hurtful words personally. Try your best to stay away from toxic people.

3. Stop putting yourself down.

You have to drop your self-deprecating humor if you want to strengthen your belief in yourself. Quit saying bad things about yourself.

4. Move forward.

Stop focusing on the past. You need to let go of past hurts and failure, and use them as motivation to succeed in life.

5. Fight procrastination.

If you constantly put off tasks, then you set yourself up for failure. If you want to strengthen your self-belief, you have to fight procrastination and start working on important tasks now.

6. Use criticism to your advantage.

While it is important not to listen to very critical people, there is some criticism you should take seriously like constructive criticism, which helps you improve yourself and your performance.

7. Identify your skills.

Everyone is good at something. You have to find that "super skill" and appreciate it. To build your self-confidence and self-belief, you have to take time to list all your good qualities. List all your talents. Are you good at writing, computer programming, or painting? When you realize you are gifted, it is easier to be confident in your abilities.

8. Learn from failure.

Failure can be a good thing because it teaches you valuable lessons to help you achieve great success in life.

9. Have realistic expectations.

When you set yourself against an unrealistically high standard, your self-belief will plummet.

10.   Remove your insecurities.

To strengthen your self-belief, you have to remove your insecurities. Accept yourself for who you are. Recognize your shortcomings and mistakes, and learn how to challenge outdated beliefs.

To build self-confidence, you have to accept one simple truth, which is: you are good enough. Accept that you are a talented and gifted person, you are valuable, and you are worthy of love and respect.

Chapter 9 - Little Acts Of Kindness

Practicing altruism and exhibiting good deeds always makes you feel better about yourself. Altruism builds confidence. Aside from that, altruism has many other psychological and physiological benefits. Altruism makes you happier and improves your emotional health. You can practice altruism by doing little acts of kindness. Here are some ways:

1. Help an old woman cross the street.

2. Give a homeless guy a hot meal.

3. Say "I love you" to your loved one, partner, or spouse.

4. Bring your assistant snacks and coffee.

5. Offer your train or bus seat to an elderly person.

6. Apologize when you make a mistake or hurt someone.

7. Give a very generous tip to a friendly and accommodating waiter.

8. Say good morning to your office security guard.

9. Smile at ten strangers daily.

10. Donate your old phones to charity.

11. Give other people genuine and sincere compliments.

12. Sincerely ask the people around you what you can do to help them.

13. Forgive someone who has wronged you.

14. Help other people carry their groceries.

15. Compliment yourself often. You deserve your own kindness, too.

16. Help a friend who is going through depression.

17. Wish someone good luck and really meant it.

18. Write thank you notes to people who have helped you and people who are nice to you.

19. Call your parents and tell them how much you love them. Tell them how grateful you are for the things they have done for you.

20. Donate one of your favorite possessions to charity.

21. Adopt a homeless cat or dog.

22. Spend a weekend teaching less fortunate kids how to read.

23. Buy flowers for your lonely neighbor.

24. Bring food to work and share it with your colleagues.

25. Bring a fruit basket to your new neighbor.

26. Give your old books to a school library.

27. Give your friend a hug when he needs it the most.

28. Let another person have the parking space.

29. Say thank you and be nice to the building janitor.

30. Throw a surprise birthday party for a friend.

31. Help a colleague with a very challenging project or task.

32. Drive a friend to the airport.

33. Give your spouse a love note.

34. Cheer someone up.

35. Give a pep talk to your demotivated colleagues.

36. Give your old clothes to fire victims.

When you do good deeds and little act of kindness, you will feel better about yourself. You will like yourself more. Kind deeds build your self-esteem and self-confidence. When you do kind deeds, you make the world a better place.

Chapter 10 - Fake It Until You Make It

Remember that confidence is just a perception. Individuals who have high self-confidence are not necessarily better or more skilled than people with poor self-confidence. The only difference is that self-confident people believe in themselves more than people with poor self-confidence.

Developing confidence usually takes time and a lot of effort. However, while waiting, you can actually feign confidence. Many psychologists recommend that you fake confidence until you become genuinely confident in yourself and your abilities.

Even if you do not feel confident yet, acting confident will yield the same benefits. Here is how you can fake confidence and eventually become genuinely confident in yourself and your abilities:

1. Imitate a confident person.

   Studies show that imitating a confident person actually makes you more confident. To develop confidence, pick a confident person and imitate his actions and disposition. It could be your boss, your sister, or a celebrity you have not met. Once you have picked the person to imitate, study his actions carefully. What makes this person confident? What are his behaviors? How does he present himself to other people?

Once you have observed your model, start imitating him. Walk like him and talk like him. You can also dress like him.

Smile often.

When you smile, you look confident. When you smile often, you are more approachable and you look sure of yourself.

2. Be shameless.

Remember that confidence is not necessarily equal to competence. However, people often equate confidence with competence. This is the reason why it is important to project confidence especially if you want to be successful in your career.

3. Dress well and groom yourself.

As mentioned earlier in this book, when you dress for success, you feel more confident. People trust you more. If you want to be successful, then it is important to dress better than even your best dressed colleague. Also, if you want to appear confident, you also have to groom yourself well. Take the time to cut your nails and trim body hairs. Make sure your hair is always in place.

4. Limit coffee, sodas, and other stimulants.

When you drink too much soda, coffee, and other stimulants, you feel jittery and anxious. When you are always fidgeting, you look unconfident.

5. Have a good posture.

If you want to look confident, then stand up straight and keep your shoulders back.

6. Make eye contact.

Try to make eye contact with random people and try your best not to look away first. When you do this, you exude confidence. You communicate to the other person that you are not easily intimidated. You show the other person that you are self-confident.

7. Lower your voice and speak slowly.

If you want to fake confidence, then you have to lower your voice and speak more slowly. Talk like you have all the time in the world. When your voice is pitchy, you seem unsure of yourself.

8. Avoid gossip.

People who gossip are insecure. If you want to fake and eventually develop confidence, then you have to speak more positively about other people and avoid gossip and back stabbing at all costs.

9. Care less about what other people say.

If you want to develop confidence, then you have to quit wondering what other people think. One day, you will realize that people are too occupied with their own lives to notice or think about you.

10.   Increase your enthusiasm.

Many people consider enthusiasm a sign of self-confidence. To fake confidence, you have to be enthusiastic. Develop a cheerful attitude.

11.   Have a firm handshake.

When you have a firm grip and handshake, you are communicating your confidence. A firm handshake lets people know you mean business.

12.   Accept compliments graciously.

Almost everyone likes to receive compliments, but people who do not have self-confidence have difficulty appreciating compliments. To project confidence, you must learn how to accept compliments. When someone compliments your work, your looks, and even your clothes simply say, "Thank you."

Fake it until you make it. When you act like a confident person, you will soon develop genuine confidence that can bring you great success in your career and in your life.

Conclusion

I hope this book was able to help you build your self-confidence and achieve great success in life and work. I hope this book helped you eliminate your self-doubt and cultivate optimism, resiliency, and other life skills needed to face life challenges. I also hope this book helped you improve your personal relationships by increasing your self-confidence.

The next step is to use this book to transform yourself and your life. Remember that the tips and strategies contained in this book are only useful and valuable if you apply them. If you find the tips and strategies in this book helpful, feel free to share them with other people. It is my goal to help as many people as possible. If you feel that your family members or your friends need to increase their self-confidence, let them read this book, as well.

Thank you and good luck!

www.ingramcontent.com/pod-product-compliance
Lightning Source LLC
Chambersburg PA
CBHW070507290526
45790CB00003B/1139